Date: 4/27/12

J 629.2222 POR
Portman, Michael,
Chargers /

WILD WHEELS

CHARGERS

By Michael Portman

Gareth Stevens
Publishing

Please visit our Web site, www.garethstevens.com. For a free color catalog of all our high-quality books, call toll free 1-800-542-2595 or fax 1-877-542-2596.

Library of Congress Cataloging-in-Publication Data

Portman, Michael, 1976-
 Chargers / Michael Portman.
    p. cm.
 Includes index.
 ISBN 978-1-4339-4740-7 (pbk.)
 ISBN 978-1-4339-4741-4 (6-pack)
 ISBN 978-1-4339-4739-1 (library binding)
 1. Dodge Charger automobile–Juvenile literature. I. Title.
 TL215.D6P67 2011
 629.222'2–dc22

                                    2010035555

First Edition

Published in 2011 by
Gareth Stevens Publishing
111 East 14th Street, Suite 349
New York, NY 10003

Copyright © 2011 Gareth Stevens Publishing

Designer: Christopher Logan
Editor: Therese Shea

Photo credits: Cover, pp. 1, 8–9, 12–13, 28–29 © Kimball Stock; Cover, pp. 2–3 (background), 30–32 (background), back cover (engine), 1, 2–32 (flame border), 4–5, 6–7, 10–11, 11 (GTO), 16–17, 21, 24, 25, 26–27 Shutterstock.com; pp. 7, 8 Car Culture/Getty Images; pp. 14–15 Dozier Mobley/Getty Images; pp. 18–19 Kevin Winter/Getty Images; pp. 20–21 iStockphoto.com; p. 22 Stan Honda/AFP/Getty Images; p. 23 Bryan Mitchell/Getty Images.

Printed in the United States of America

CPSIA compliance information: Batch #CW11GS: For further information contact Gareth Stevens, New York, New York at 1-800-542-2595.

CONTENTS

Words in the glossary appear in **bold** type the first time they are used in the text.

Flexing Their Muscles

In the 1960s, a new type of car muscled its way onto American streets. It was called a muscle car. A muscle car is midsized, affordable, and features a powerful engine. Although Dodge had been producing fast cars with powerful engines, their **designs** were considered old-fashioned. Dodge knew they had to do something different to compete with other companies' muscle cars.

To keep manufacturing cheap and simple, most car companies use a practice called **platform sharing**. A company can build several models that look different, but share the same basic structure. Platform sharing allowed Dodge to quickly create the Charger.

The assembly line is another way for car companies to produce cars quickly. Cars travel down a line while workers put parts in place until the car is complete.

INSIDE THE MACHINE

The Dodge brand has been around for many years. It was founded in 1914 by two brothers, Horace and John Dodge. In 1928, Dodge was sold to the Chrysler Corporation, now known as the Chrysler Group. The Chrysler Group currently owns the Chrysler, Dodge, and Jeep brands.

First Generation (1966 – 1967)

The first generation, or class, of Charger was anything but traditional. It had a roof that sloped down in the back—a style called a fastback. It also had headlights hidden in the **grille**. The Dodge Charger was built using the Chrysler B-body platform, which meant that it was bigger than most muscle cars. To power a car this large, Dodge offered a variety of engine choices, including the powerful 426 Hemi.

Can you see this Charger's headlights? The hidden headlights made this Dodge stand out.

The 1966 model wasn't an instant success, but it sold well. Therefore, few changes were made to the 1967 model. Competition was fierce in the muscle-car market. When the 1967 model sold poorly, Dodge knew it was time to make a change.

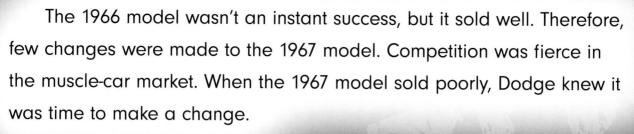

INSIDE THE MACHINE

The inside of the 1966–1967 Dodge Charger was considered state-of-the-art. It featured four separate seats called bucket seats, and the rear seats folded down for extra room! The instrument panel consisted of four dials that glowed brightly in the dark.

bucket seats

Second Generation (1968–1970)

The second Charger generation shared the same B-body as the first, but it was a much different car. The **fenders** curved around the tires, and the body was longer. The whole car seemed to lean forward, ready to go. The Charger looked fast even when it was standing still!

But what good is a muscle car if it only looks fast? In 1968, Dodge introduced a high-performance Charger called the Charger R/T, which stands for Road/Track. The Charger R/T featured heavy-duty brakes and **suspension** as well as wider tires. Engine choices, including the 440 Magnum and the 426 Hemi, offered plenty of **horsepower**.

This sleek 1968 Dodge Charger turned heads as it cruised down the highway.

The Dodge Charger offered features we take for granted today, such as cruise control and air conditioning. One thing it didn't offer was good gas mileage. Depending on the engine, a second-generation Charger could get between 8 and 14 miles (13 and 23 km) per gallon on the highway. That's a big difference compared to a modern Charger, which can get up to 26 miles (42 km) per gallon!

440 Magnum engine

If the second-generation Charger is considered the best-looking Charger, the 1969 Charger is thought by many to be the best overall. It looked similar to the 1968 model but featured a center divider in the grille and redesigned taillights. The 1969 Charger was also the first Dodge to offer a power sunroof.

The 1970 model was the last of the second generation. Dodge did little but increase the Charger's length by 1 inch (2.5 cm). The center grille divider was removed and a bumper now surrounded the grille. The 1968 and 1969 Chargers sold well, but the 1970 model wasn't nearly as successful.

Dodge made only small changes to the second-generation Charger, mostly around the grille. They knew Charger fans liked the overall design.

INSIDE THE MACHINE

The shape of the second-generation Charger looks similar to a glass cola bottle. This shape was very popular in muscle cars during the 1960s and 1970s. Many of the bottle-styled muscle cars looked very similar. For instance, a 1969 Pontiac GTO could be mistaken for a 1969 Dodge Charger.

GTO Judge

Dodge 500

During the 1960s and 1970s, cars competing in NASCAR (National Association for Stock Car Auto Racing) races were very similar to those sold across the country. Dodge hoped for racing success with the 1969 Charger, but it had some serious problems on the track. Its design caused it to be unstable and unsafe at high speeds. Dodge made some changes to the grille and the rear window.

The new design was called the Charger 500. The Charger 500 won a few races in 1969, but wasn't as successful as Dodge had hoped. Fortunately, Dodge had another trick up its sleeve.

This 1969 Dodge Charger 500 had a powerful Hemi engine, designed for NASCAR racing.

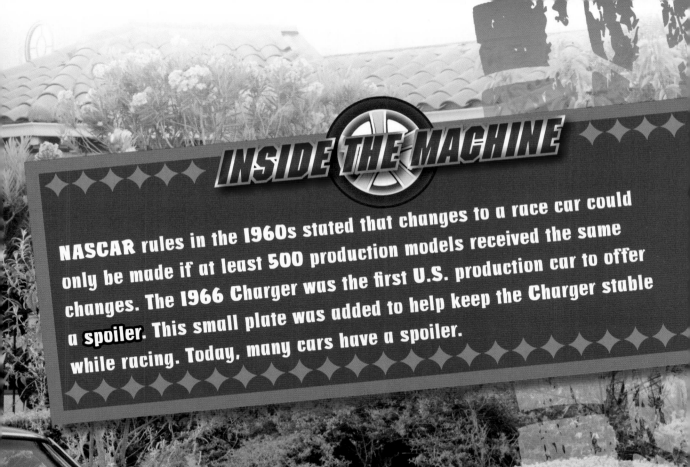

INSIDE THE MACHINE

NASCAR rules in the 1960s stated that changes to a race car could only be made if at least 500 production models received the same changes. The 1966 Charger was the first U.S. production car to offer a **spoiler**. This small plate was added to help keep the Charger stable while racing. Today, many cars have a spoiler.

Charger Daytona

The problem with the Charger 500 wasn't the engine—it was the shape. The Charger Daytona took the 500's body and added a long, wedge-shaped grille that made it more **aerodynamic**. The Daytona was one of the most distinctive cars in NASCAR. Its only purpose was to win races, and that's exactly what it did! The Charger Daytona won its very first race in 1969, the Talladega 500.

This Charger Daytona, driven by Buddy Baker, was the first car to reach 200 miles (322 km) per hour in NASCAR.

In 1970, the Charger Daytona became the first car in NASCAR history to complete a lap at more than 200 miles (322 km) per hour! Charger Daytonas raced until 1971, when NASCAR rule changes targeted cars with winged spoilers.

INSIDE THE MACHINE

The most noticeable thing about the Charger Daytona was the 23-inch (58-cm) rear spoiler. Since computers weren't used to design cars during the 1960s, Dodge had to use **wind tunnels** to test the aerodynamics of their cars. After much trial and error, the giant winged spoiler was found to be the best design.

On Screen

The second-generation Dodge Charger has been featured in many television programs, movies, and video games. The most well-known is the General Lee, a 1969 Charger made famous by the TV show *The Dukes of Hazzard*. From 1979 to 1985, viewers tuned in each week to watch the General Lee jump over trains, rivers, even houses, and drive away without a scratch!

The General Lee Dodge Charger is one of the most recognizable cars in the world!

Of course, a Dodge Charger can't really do all those things. Professional stunt drivers destroyed one or two Chargers per episode! The exact number of Chargers used on the show isn't known, but it's said to be between 256 and 321.

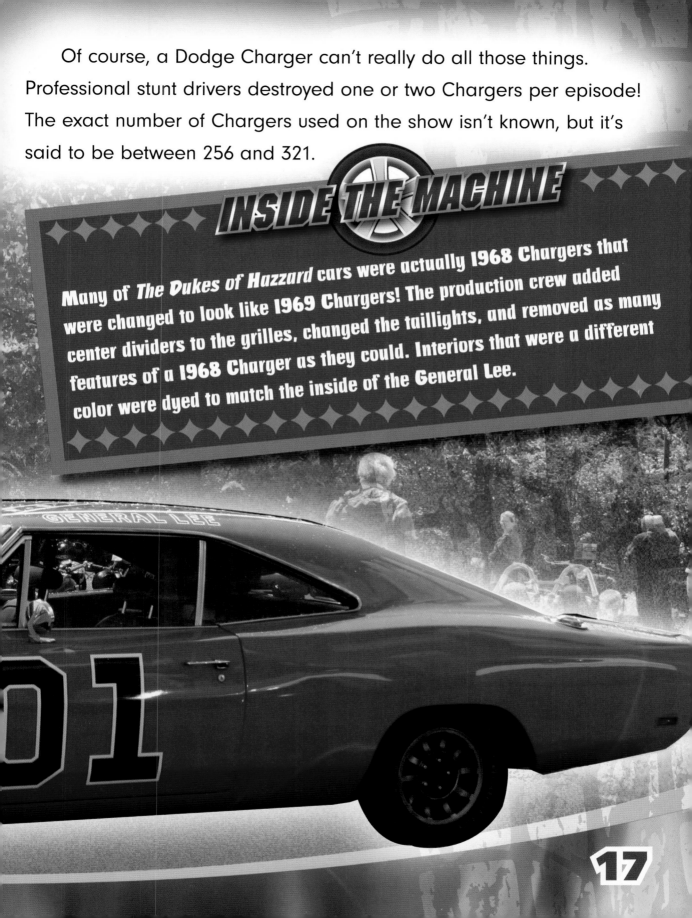

INSIDE THE MACHINE

Many of *The Dukes of Hazzard* cars were actually 1968 Chargers that were changed to look like 1969 Chargers! The production crew added center dividers to the grilles, changed the taillights, and removed as many features of a 1968 Charger as they could. Interiors that were a different color were dyed to match the inside of the General Lee.

Money problems during the last season of *The Dukes of Hazzard* forced the show's producers to use old scenes as well as miniature cars. Today, less than 20 of the original General Lees are still in existence. The General Lee returned to the screen in the 2005 movie version of *The Dukes of Hazzard*.

On the big screen, a 1968 Dodge Charger R/T was featured in a famous chase scene from the movie *Bullitt*. A 1969 Charger, modified to look like a 1970 model, was used in the movie *The Fast and the Furious*. Fans of racing games get a chance to drive a Charger in the Xbox 360 game *Project Gotham Racing 4*.

The popularity of *The Dukes of Hazzard* has led many people to change their Dodge Chargers to make them look like the General Lee. Of course, not owning a Dodge Charger hasn't stopped some people from making similar modifications. Other cars, trucks, vans, lawn mowers, bicycles, and just about anything with wheels has been made to look like the General Lee!

This Charger R/T was just one of the classic cars adapted for high performance and head-turning style for *The Fast and the Furious* movie.

End of an Era

In 1971, Dodge completely redesigned the Charger for its third generation, making it shorter, wider, and curvier. These changes were popular. In fact, the 1973 Charger was the best-selling Charger! However, by 1974, customers were more interested in comfort than power. Cars were getting bigger, but the engines were getting less powerful. The muscle-car era was coming to an end.

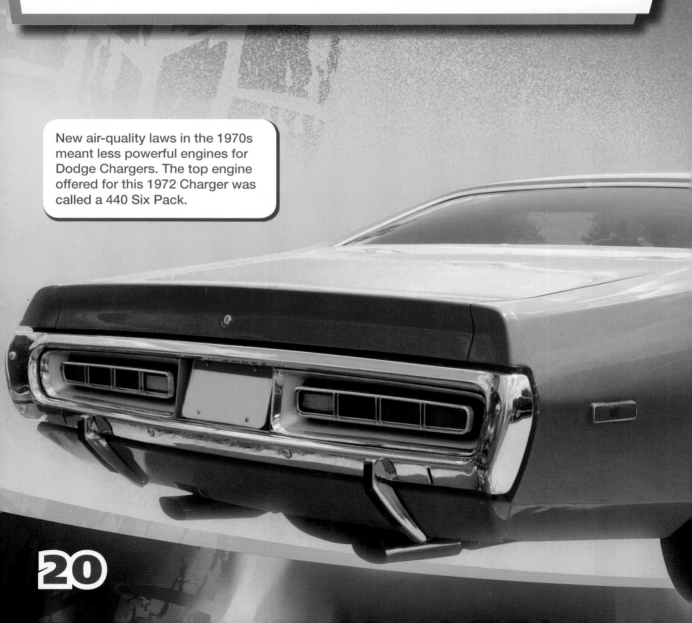

New air-quality laws in the 1970s meant less powerful engines for Dodge Chargers. The top engine offered for this 1972 Charger was called a 440 Six Pack.

The fourth-generation Dodge Charger lasted from 1975 until 1977. These Chargers were big, boxy, and slow. The Charger was no longer a muscle car! Sales were poor, and Dodge decided to make another change. This time, instead of redesigning the Charger, Dodge decided to replace it in 1978.

INSIDE THE MACHINE

The fourth-generation Charger was the last Charger to use the B-body platform. Chrysler ended production of the B-body in 1979. Fourteen different cars were built on the B-body platform during its 17 years of existence.

Modern Muscle

The Dodge Charger returned in 1982 for its fifth generation. It was nothing like previous Chargers. Instead, it was a small **hatchback** with **front-wheel drive**. It wasn't a bad little car, but it certainly wasn't a muscle car! In 1987, Dodge stopped production of the Charger for the second time. It would be a few more years before a new Charger would appear.

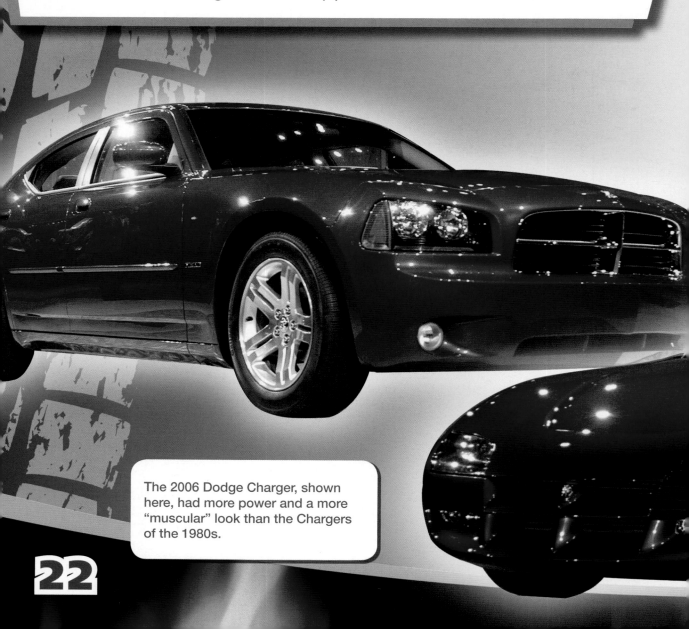

The 2006 Dodge Charger, shown here, had more power and a more "muscular" look than the Chargers of the 1980s.

The all-new Dodge Charger returned in 2006. The new Charger was built on Chrysler's LX platform. Many fans of the classic Chargers weren't happy that the sixth generation had four doors. They were hoping for a two-door **coupe**. Even so, the new Charger was a success.

INSIDE THE MACHINE

Charger fans were excited in 1999 when a Dodge Charger concept car began making appearances at auto shows. Sleek and curvy, it looked like a modern Charger Daytona. Unfortunately, it was never produced.

This 1999 Charger concept car was powered by natural gas!

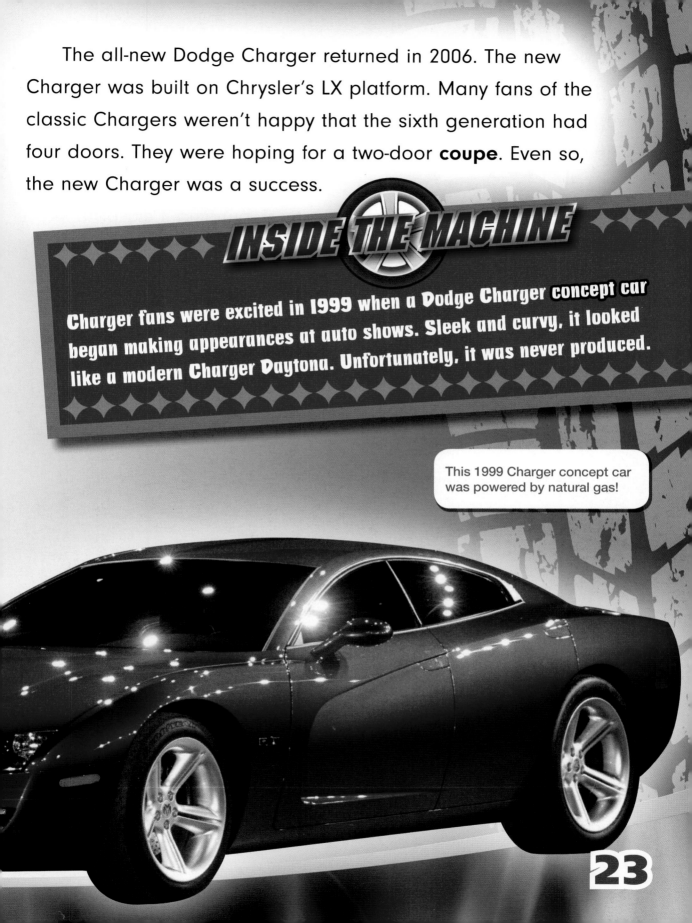

In addition to getting much better gas mileage than earlier Chargers, the sixth-generation Charger is safe. It earned the government's safest "crash rating." The new Charger is fast, too. A Charger with a Hemi can go 0 to 60 miles (97 km) per hour in 6 seconds! Dodge has no plans to discontinue the Charger anytime soon. The 2011 Charger will be redesigned, bringing it closer to its muscle-car roots.

The Chargers of the 2000s don't look like classic Chargers, but they offer powerful engines for muscle-car lovers.

The return of the Charger also meant a return to NASCAR. Unlike previous NASCAR Chargers, current ones are almost completely different from the models sold at dealerships.

INSIDE THE MACHINE

Every NASCAR race car is built entirely for speed and safety. Drivers are surrounded by a cage made of steel tubes to protect them if the car crashes or rolls over. Each car also has a roof hatch to allow the driver to escape during an emergency. There is even a TV camera inside to allow fans to see what a race looks like from inside the car!

Police Charger

When a police force chooses its cars, it looks for ones that are both fast and safe. Many police forces across the country use Dodge Chargers. Chargers used by police include better suspension and safety features than those made for regular customers.

The Dodge Chargers used by police forces are able to handle a variety of driving conditions.

Dodge Chargers are already heavy. Sirens, lights, radios, electronics, and police equipment make them even heavier. The ability to quickly and safely stop a heavy car that's traveling at high speeds is important. The heavy-duty brakes used in police Chargers allow the car to stop much more quickly than other police cars.

INSIDE THE MACHINE

The Dodge Charger can easily reach speeds of 150 miles (240 km) per hour, making it one of the fastest police cars on the road. In speed tests, a police Charger with a Hemi easily beats police cars from other companies!

Collectibles

The first-generation and second-generation Dodge Chargers are still popular today. People take great pride in restoring and displaying their Chargers at car shows and exhibits across the country. Classic Dodge Chargers are also valuable. A Dodge Charger R/T that sold for $4,000 in 1969 can now sell for over $50,000!

The 1969 Dodge Charger R/T SE included special details such as brightly trimmed foot pedals. It's still a popular choice for collectors.

INSIDE THE MACHINE

The 1969 Dodge Charger Daytona is an extremely rare car. This model was only produced for 1 year, and just over 500 were built. Today, one can sell for over $300,000! The Dodge Charger Daytona name returned in 2006, but unlike the original Charger Daytona, it looked just like a regular Charger.

Glossary

aerodynamic: having a shape that improves airflow around a car to increase its speed

concept car: a car built to show a new design and features that may one day be used in cars sold to the public

coupe: a two-door car with one section for the seat and another for storage space

cruise control: a device in a car that maintains a speed chosen by the driver

design: the pattern or shape of something

fender: any of the corner parts of the body of a car, especially those that surround the wheels

front-wheel drive: a system of moving a car that uses the engine to power the front wheels only

grille: a metal screen on the front of a car that allows cool air into the engine

hatchback: a car design in which the trunk lid is replaced with a door that opens upwards and usually includes the rear window

horsepower: a measurement of an engine's power

platform sharing: using the same structure and many of the same parts to build a variety of different cars

spoiler: a wing-shaped device attached to the back of the car to improve airflow and stability

suspension: a system of springs and other devices on a car that reduces the shaking and bumping caused by uneven road surfaces

wind tunnel: a tunnel in which a current of air is blown around a car to determine its aerodynamic qualities

For More Information

Books

Leffingwell, Randy, and Darwin Holmstrom. *Muscle: America's Legendary Performance Cars*. St. Paul, MN: Motorbooks, 2006.

Mueller, Mike. *The Complete Book of Dodge and Plymouth Muscle*. Minneapolis, MN: MBI Publishing Company and Motorbooks, 2009.

Poolos, Jamie. *Wild About Muscle Cars*. New York, NY: Rosen Publishing, 2008.

Web Sites

Collisionkids.org
www.collisionkids.org
Learn about cars by playing games and completing related projects.

Dodge History
www.edmunds.com/dodge/history.html
Learn about the history of the Dodge company, and find links to information about Chargers.

What's Inside: Muscle Cars
musclecars.howstuffworks.com
Learn about the mechanics of muscle cars, and see some classic examples.

Index